MYTHICAL MATCHUPS

# PEGASUS VS. UNICORN

BY A.J. SAUTTER

CAPSTONE PRESS
a capstone imprint

Published by Capstone Press, an imprint of Capstone
1710 Roe Crest Drive, North Mankato, Minnesota 56003
capstonepub.com

Copyright © 2026 by Capstone. All rights reserved. No part of this publication may be reproduced in whole or in part, or stored in a retrieval system, or transmitted in any form or by any means, electronic, mechanical, photocopying, recording, or otherwise, without written permission of the publisher.

Library of Congress Cataloging-in-Publication Data is available on the Library of Congress website.

ISBN: 9798875255649 (hardcover)
ISBN: 9798875255595 (paperback)
ISBN: 9798875255601 (ebook PDF)

Summary: Who would come out on top in a head-to-head battle between a pegasus and a unicorn?

Editorial Credits
Editor: Alison Deering; Designer: Bobbie Nuytten; Media Researcher: Svetlana Zhurkin; Production Specialist: Katy LaVigne

Image Credits
Dreamstime: Ateliersommerland, 16, Corey A Ford, 5, 6, 8, 9, 10, 20, 21, 22, 26, 29, Digitalstormcinema, 14–15, Obsidianfantasy, 11, Pavel Durov, 19, Ratpack2, 7, Simone Gatterwe, 24, Tudorpopaart, 12–13; Shutterstock: Blagorodez, cover (light beam), 27 (magic light), Catmando, cover (unicorn), 18, 23, 27 (unicorn), Daniel Eskridge, cover (pegasus), 4, Ellerslie, 28, Ian Luck, 17, klyaksun, cover (light orb), lovelyday12, cover (bottom back), Tan_supa, cover (top back), Viktoriia Bondarenko, 25, Wirestock Creators, back cover, 2–3, 30–31

Any additional websites and resources referenced in this book are not maintained, authorized, or sponsored by Capstone. All product and company names are trademarks™ or registered® trademarks of their respective holders.

Printed and bound in China. 6459

# Table of Contents



Words in **bold** are in the glossary.

# A Meeting in the Meadow

A winged creature flies high in the sky. It's a pegasus! It swoops down to land in a **meadow**. The fresh grass will make a tasty snack.

A unicorn steps into the clearing. It spots the pegasus. The unicorn lowers its head and charges.

It's a **mythical** creature showdown! Who will come out on top?

# Majestic Beasts

Pegasi appear in ancient myths. These winged creatures sometimes became friends with people. But they usually lived on their own in the wild.

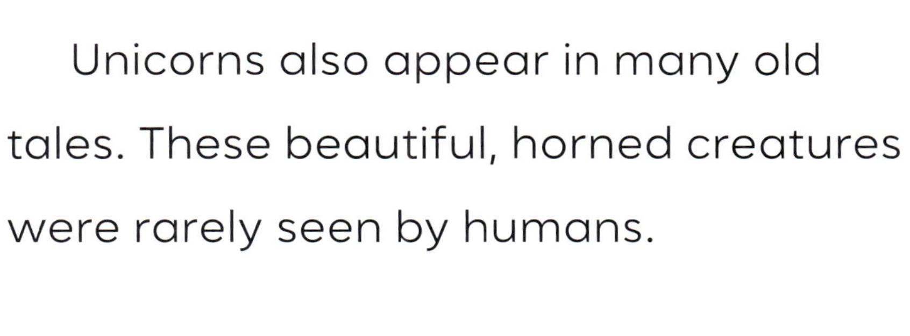

Unicorns also appear in many old tales. These beautiful, horned creatures were rarely seen by humans.

What would happen if these two beasts met face-to-face?

# Meet the Rivals

## PEGASUS

STRONG, FEATHERED WINGS—used for flying

SHARP EYESIGHT—used for spotting objects on the ground during flight

MANE AND TAIL—used for changing direction during flight

MUSCULAR BODY—used for ramming enemies

STRONG LEGS—used for charging or kicking enemies

UNICORN
HORN—used for magical attacks and stabbing enemies
SHARP EYESIGHT—used for spotting intruders
MUSCULAR BODY—used for ramming enemies
STRONG LEGS—used for charging or kicking enemies

# Wild and Free

Most pegasi live by themselves in forests or on wide **plains**. Very few have ever been **tamed**.

Pegasi are **intelligent**. They will attack a wicked person. But they may befriend someone who is kind and respectful.

# Private and Proud

Unicorns live mainly in thick forests. They sometimes visit small clearings to **graze**. But they typically stay hidden among the trees.

Unicorns rarely make friends. They avoid humans completely. But a few are friends with elves or fairies who respect nature.

# Big, Fast Flyers

Pegasi are like horses but larger. Most are about 12 feet (3.7 meters) long. They stand 10 to 12 feet (3 to 3.7 m) tall.

Pegasi have feathered wings. They stretch up to 25 feet (7.6 m) wide. These wings help pegasi fly fast. They can fly up to 50 miles (80 kilometers) per hour.

# Swift and Strong

Unicorns are about the size of a horse. An adult unicorn is about 8 to 9 feet (2.4 to 2.7 m) long. They are about 7 feet (2.1 m) tall.

Unicorns have strong legs and muscles. They run about 50 miles (80 km) per hour. They can run many miles without growing tired.

# Powerful Flight

A pegasus's wings are its main weapon. They allow it to swoop down from above and attack. They also help it **dodge** and spin to avoid midair attacks.

Pegasi don't fight well on the ground. They can't turn easily. Their wings make them clumsy.

# Strong Horns

Unicorns are known for their magical horns. These are usually 2 to 2.5 feet (0.6 to 0.8 m) long. Horns are used to stab at enemies. They can also unleash a powerful blast of magical energy.

If a unicorn loses its horn, it becomes very weak. Until the horn grows back, the unicorn is defenseless.

# Surprise Attackers

Pegasi are fantastic fighters in the air. They fly high to look for enemies. Then they silently swoop down for a surprise attack.

A pegasus will kick or ram its **foe** from above. The goal is to injure the enemy and knock it down. Then the pegasus soars into the air for another attack.

# Fearsome Defenders

Unicorns fiercely defend their homes. If threatened, a unicorn will lower its head and horn. It will charge to chase an enemy away.

If that doesn't work, a unicorn will use magic. It will blast the enemy with energy from its horn. The attack forces the foe to flee. The invader will lose any memory of the meeting.

# Fierce Forest Fight

In the meadow, the pegasus sees the unicorn charging. It spreads its wings and launches into the air. The unicorn's horn barely misses!

The unicorn rears up and kicks. But the pegasus is out of reach. It swoops and dives. The unicorn is ready. Its horn glows with magical light.

Which of these beautiful beasts will win this forest fight?

# Who Will Win?

Unicorns don't like intruders. They will fiercely protect their forest homes. Pegasi are fantastic flyers. Few creatures can beat them in the air.

Compare each creature's strengths and weaknesses. Then decide who would win a mythical matchup!

| | PEGASUS | UNICORN |
|---|---|---|
| SIZE | 12 feet (3.7 m) long; 10 to 12 feet (3 to 3.7 m) tall; 25-foot (7.6 m) wingspan | 8 to 9 feet (2.4 to 2.7 m) long; 7 feet (2.1 m) tall |
| SPEED | 50 miles (80 km) per hour flying | 50 miles (80 km) per hour running |
| HABITAT | forests and wide plains | forests with grassy meadows |
| WEAPONS | sharp eyesight, strong legs, powerful wings | sharp eyesight, strong legs, magical horn |
| FIGHTING STYLE | surprise air attacks, kicking or ramming attacks | charging stab attacks, powerful kicking, magical energy blasts |

# GLOSSARY

**dodge** (DOJ)—to avoid something by moving quickly

**foe** (FOH)—an enemy

**graze** (GRAYZ)—to eat grass and other plants

**intelligent** (in-TEL-ih-juhnt)—able to think, understand, and solve problems

**meadow** (MED-oh)—a big, usually low area of land that is mostly covered with grass

**mythical** (MITH-ih-kuhl)—imaginary or not real

**plain** (PLEYN)—a large, flat area of land with few trees

**tame** (TEYM)—trained to live with or be useful to people

# READ MORE

Hansen, Grace. *Unicorns*. Minneapolis: Abdo Kids Jumbo, 2023.

Meister, Cari. *Unicorns*. North Mankato, MN: Picture Window Books, 2020.

Sanderson, Whitney. *Pegasus*. Minneapolis: Abdo Publishing, 2022.

# INTERNET SITES

*Britannica Kids: Pegasus*
kids.britannica.com/kids/article/Pegasus/353609

*Britannica Kids: Unicorn*
kids.britannica.com/kids/article/unicorn/390060

*Kiddle: Pegasus Facts for Kids*
kids.kiddle.co/Pegasus

*Kiddle: Unicorn Facts for Kids*
kids.kiddle.co/Unicorn

# INDEX



# ABOUT THE AUTHOR

A.J. Sautter is an author and editor of dozens of cool books for young readers. He enjoys books about aliens, sports, magic tricks, and especially fantastic creatures. When not battling dragons and ogres in his wild imagination, he enjoys cheering for the Minnesota Vikings and exploring the woods with his goofy, lovable dogs.